# The Frame of a Book

# A Frame
# of the Book

Poems

# Erin Mouré

Published in 1999 by
House of Anansi Press Limited
34 Lesmill Road
Toronto, ON
M3B 2T6
Tel. (416) 445-3333
Fax (416) 445-5967
www.anansi.ca
E-mail Customer.Service@ccmailgw.genpub.com

CANADIAN CATALOGUING IN PUBLICATION DATA

Mouré, Erin, 1955–
    Frame of the book

Poems.
ISBN 0-88784-632-7

I. Title.

PS8576.O96F72 1999      C811'.54      C98-933056-7
PR9199.3.M68F72 1999

Printed and bound in Canada

*House of Anansi Press gratefully acknowledges the Canada Council for*
*the Arts, the Government of Canada through the Book Publishing Industry*
*Development Program (BPIDP), and the Ontario Arts Council for their*
*support of our publishing program.*

# CONTENTS

## An abrasion Series

## The Her Sensorium

*Je vais bien je vais bien je vois de moins en moins*
*Quelle joie d'être vivante*

Michael Palmer, *Série Baudelaire*
(trans. Emmanuel Hocquard and Philippe Mikriammos)


*Et qu'est-ce que le livre sinon la longue préparation*
*du corps aux mots enfouis de son absence?*

Edmond Jabès, *Le Livre des ressemblances*

# An abrasion Series

# Thrum

There were charmed trespass we couldn't send

Gates that trembled over *omega*

Fortuity sembling a fond polestar

In our house a cuisine
spelled wrong
Horned in sideways

Trumped-up temerity
to endless *leave*
"you old conniver"

Where indigenous is a heartstroke from picturesque

Her fond melody near me

When I craved melody's end, anoint
inscriptive


%

Unable -- henceforth --
To decry "facticity" in the line
where she entered through a sound door
the door frame squared off
perfectly
"& all that"

Fortuity is a candle that eludes regret?
Waiting for "both of us" to blunder through
(a doorway)
Basically -- impetuous --

%

Meeting, in a word, our homonyms
of exemplary endeavour
To wake up thinking
"the virus mendacious in a tomb"
the dreamed dog soft in my arms
skinless red, a meat curmudgeon
To dream a face is to
mesmerize infinitely
Whose curious soft eyes everywhere

thrum


%

As if a wilfulness infinitesimally forestalls regret
forestalls absence
"A dog fallen over sideways in a hug's fierce
hegemony"

a tune

sung aloud for "Irish voices"
meaning "there is a lilt"

"walking toward me laughing on Salem at Bloor"
"a gethsemane of indigence stole us"
"Eddy picking up *4 on 2* in the 1364"*
"K's smile"

a neat reasonable blade of sunlight
's transversal

objectic
eidem

---

* *impossible, "in fact"*

4

%

Which becomes gradually more narrational.
Out of the heart,
which has been dispensed with

*or not*

Or eased into joy
eased into "warm company"
then left suddenly alone
Looking up from the pale loam of the chest to the window

where they say
                    "a fact of it"

                    "the world lies*"


%

As if an the opus corrupted enmity
Saying "gafas de sol"
would you believe it
at such a moment
(it's a gay life ain't it)

"gafas de sol"

---

* confabulate    charms    trespass    endures

%

or frail misericordia
Did they want lament  (I don't think so)

*To disseminate*

# Gust

The invisible proposition survived as content
After the fins were eaten or laid down, the tablecloth gently

billowing

& our knees beneath that

was serenity a

vocabulary or doubt


A smooth haze westerly scudded – – –
How do you know
To say here

is

or – – –


Palimpsest a settled Rome vernacular
Pulling its luscious cord her grandest soutane fell

an immense cloth addressed with tender stitching
that later looked "like chives"

we rolled over into it
this every girl must sate or do
this every girl must astonish or tonality

spur

trigger a

lip, sheen, mar, glossalial, glea

Otro imbroglio
a silence wept here it was so tentative[°]
or femur gaze

Thus "I" became a transitive being
transition appealed me & I wandered thusly
irremedial

or femur gaze a lamp above my hair does shine
would that its treble named me

would that its field a pair ensure


– – –
– – –
an apparitional motion – – –
– – –
       – – –




To repeat a word so much infests a coil or troll
a mete or fender
a groat or inner fey
a flick or tremble
hone east tea

where I touched yr shoulder spoke into the bone

A ship rose there
We steered by it

Faient pleasure named us


---

[°] "beautiful"

Inside yr arm      synecdoche

"were" heard as "wear"

We were alone there almost speaking

one syllable did inure or disobey

addendum data clarity

nadie


A scent of – – –
or
let you decide if absence' reconnaissance
Again I must say "tentative"[ø] in this formulation

*There is* has been a lure

Can I say this too or is it added slowly
a confection

abeyant synonym agreement hologr

meu lar meu lar


Event establish
mediodía mi amor

– – – protect us

Let others shift their weapons sleeping
(an English sentenc

Fain would ever we inure

---

[ø] "beautiful"

# 14 Descriptions of Trees

*for h.z.l.*

I

My old habit attenuates an inner liquor or sigh.

Description sets up a distribution of effect
animals' furred ruffs may also cherish
Description demands its transformation to the letters,
the world did not conform to description
with immediacy

as light is solved. *"When I wake up, you are still
sleeping."* The present tense herein invests

a simultaneity of affect
Ameliorates an absence


2

But the problems of description continue
The various sub-scopes of envision forest an extreme,
or obligation


3

Largely a travesty can possess,

or murmur

A night with no brink

trope assignation making us plural

who "us" are

willed places destine

We hesitant before longing

## 4

Now someone has uttered the word "Boltanski" in a yellow kitchen
Is this the form our grief has taken

A wide memory is ours, is ours
A terrace *très jaune* to be traversed before waking

Sirop of such trees, a clamber out
of sleep or waking

A far journey is ours, is ours

this much is clear from the terrible story


## 5

Their leaves red words for
Impediment a hoarse or cry
An imagine does indicate or where
False gestures submerge us


## 6

Astonish me a core of blood

Trying to stick in this course to the "believable"

our ephemeron does so compel me

The present tense is my imbroglio

my nymphic ore

dilatory or sonorous

a mediate or

## 7

Writing the lines called *Grief, or Sweetness*
& wanting your green-hazedname

hawks

## CODA (replaces 8–14)

I have told you the story of a small red shoe
Most of the time it is irreplaceable

A far journey is ours, is ours

That much is clear from the terrible story

It is the saga of a small red shoe
the journey itself is unmistakable

Most of the time it is a word that shatters all

That much is clear from the trembulous forage

Now someone has uttered the host "Boltanski" in a metal kitchen
Is this the tree of grief mistaken

the marsh outside yr eye & hand where hawks did wander
their shadows moved you

in that metal kitchen

. . .

. . .

That much is clear from the torporous alloy

Most of the time it is a shoe that shatters all *

---

* But the problems of investiture continue. Its travesty can presume a fervour. Most of
the time the world does not respond to such description. Most of the time a word's
will shatters all.

# Astro's House of Ripey Lyrick, or *the Features*

document3

A body appears, agitating being entirely

anatomy is "not to doubt"

An isthmus

traced against my wrist looped upward

agitating anatomy entirely

*Astro's House of Ripey Lyrick*

document1

Looking outward through the throngs of a strength message

Inventivity her prolect

Her foregone impetus to bloom

\*

*A face coalesces where a face is, I will never lose you among the features*

Ontology's gesture oh sensation she is wearing that strap again

document5

A ligament conveys "there is a torn"

O that ripey lyrick, suddenly seized
"to bear a ruffed nomenclature"

Cutting it open along the red haunch, she ecsta–ic

Two hermetic girls' indigence is on the wane

To blunt me with your wield in my surge
box of girlish feeling

& call out the lost *t* ascensions




document1

Vascular comfort or "imaginable" a prolected Kim

Invect her configuration's prolonged deploy *in me*

The mark left "us" where a scandalized one has

vanished

Waking up to the noise down the road (her right ear)

The whirr from the grain dryer * *

document4

What if: a pentimiento of a charm's gaze

Where a scandalized one has now surmounted

the trimmed mound of far lexia

mitt or weal upon a page

Where the vanished *doubled* is pur caesura

Beside myself, *you are*, a word "semblaient"...

Erosion Theory Coil Theory Maintenance Device:

| EROSION | THEORY |
|---|---|
| SURGE | THEORY |
| MAINTENANCE | DEVICE |

# The Red Archive (her harsh or perfect mechanism)

In flux imagination
her fortitude's appendage wreaks
Is sordid of wane particulars
my labial promiscuity
my labial touch her circuit widens
homeograph allows to mete out thrum possibility
Is there a wreaked harbour bid or taken
A vase portrait shows caress
has been established
its fascicle or herb tempera
makes portrait possible over unearthed time

If our slant endogamy cd but endure

------------------------------------------------------------------------

a)  In fact, what stability
    depends on,
    an allure

b)  Her fetishized right ear
    before hand

c)  An allure before a hospital
    craves in
    Immense diencephalon of home

self suppliant mechanism
(idea of pliancy)

harsh science mood
(idea of redundancy)

cell theory or technograph
(idea of portent)

(idea of coalesce)
(time photo of kissy smearr)

I actively searched out corruption
The continued use of this instrument
its red archive

where subjects come into being
or not
The body has its parts again (to grieve)
some are strappable

we discard after the detonations

wash off & conduct employ
aggrandize with such fondness
Your metrical drift of a category "she"
Integrally bound
I actively searched out conducive practice
Scuzziness to forget
to accent

------------------------------------------------------------------

The inability to sustain a home
an unfortunate result of narrative

A bees tempography Orpheus abjure

Talk envious to wit induction's
faint impediment or gleam
She pulls her seam aside its lozenge
flourish

Incense intesmal ortitude amurr
Or coffee in a white glass spurred on

her impale glistens
touched or solitude amassed this
touch or finger to repeat

at variable speed
Waist-high to prevent establish

& caress endure which then releases
sputum a feeling intellect entails
her opaque & gorgeous fluid mechanism

a transferral of insects across a
boudoir of doubt
where

"some are strappable"
some endure the pleasantry of inject
some utter platitudes to infer a laugh
waist-high in these grasses

To wake beside her "right ear"
A courteous & forgiving mechanism

in fact forbade
(she forebade it)

isolate force
contagion to adore, delect
whose mouth parts hold that fond archive

| | |
|---|---|
| Whose was endured | my rough semantic gleam |
| operate her | wiles I heretofore ensue |
| | |
| A lilt compels | her metal to my bone |
| a homeo | erotic mechanism |
| | |
| cathect a trill | to assimilate |
| some possibles | touched us "absolutely" |
| | |
| Swayed light a | harsh or perfect mechanism |
| her shoulder true in memory | *her right ear* |

the our episode

---

# BUT NO PLACE ON EARTH IS WITHOUT ITS* BEAUTY.

*caer

# Report from the Interior, a Swan Song*

Tremendum.

The thorax of a bird. Soft stroke of the chest. Head caplet. Pale rope
air. Struggle over particles of sleep, impassable, smallish white hair
grows the skull predisposed. Amalgam sleep, patch neural, small
teeming slices. A public figure is history to the ear. By her ear, these
pale hairs. A bird's ear? Its head cocked & bulged eye, water & gas.
*Angelikē*. Suit jacket. Her overcoat full of cold startled air;

---

* "It is impossible to make any real sense of what happened." *(the judge's words,
repeated here in memory of John Ryan Turner, aged 3 yrs. 9 mos. at his death, from a
wasting syndrome due to a lack of parental love)*

Torsional

Emblem small wonder's socket. Love of these flags. *White Rose.* To
touch her ear, warm where she lies, breathing. A pump noise. The
ground lately with its blue oil, rubbed earth. Strings of pointed flags
flapped downward, triangles of these flags. Slice magazine a
downward layer. Heat release. One hole pale lit beneath track of.
One hoist. Garagiste. Jacket pulled up at the neck, orderly hospice,
releases old upholstery, dragnet, a smell of car air

Trochar (her mouth)

Where well-dressed means "against the cold", the bate of the breath
silent, a snow light shorn. To stand stare intent at the tipped bare
branches, white ache of snow & no other colour, impedance of cold
entering the jacket. Her hair on the pillow countable white bent up a
bit. Lean whisper or gaze. Skin pale imprinted with. Listen to her, O
ache of these tiny willow buds layer on layer. *Anastazja*. A stony
immigration, worn smooth

The mouth.

Hot wind ribbed into the curled chest warm stuck with old cloth. Ribs
of cloth twist strips. Dry. Open at the wrists a quietude, bliss white
keys. Cold touch of the white keys on the child's hand. Front of the
Mendelssohn so cherry oaken. White hair a sheet endeavours. Stroke
this hair, top of. Warm inner paw of light. Facsimilitic breathing.
Toreadore. Shadow of the girl. Her. Young leap abstinent. The
overcoat with steel air, flooded open

Tenebrae

O the wide Missouri now

O across that light, small cocked bird its light head & dwelling
breakup shorn spring

We fell into the river

She remembers

Personable, they say, child climbing out of the

Her child's leg well-dressed

jammed in the ice floe

She looks to me with pale blue translucence. Ice

her sister pulls

Leg of old corduroy sodden & icy

against an unwitted darkness

her dream a

a soft snow

You pulled me upward, she said

*It was not me, I said*, stroking her hair & leaning close, her
breath was so damaged it was a bridge a thread a way she had of
moving her head once, l'orgueil, comprenez-vous

You pulled me upward, she said

*Yes, I said*

I smell your jacket, she said

*Yes? I said*

It smells like the White Rose station when we were young

*When _I_ was young, I said. You were grown up already –*

No, I was young too, she said

Put your coat on , she said, so as I can smell it

*Yes, I said*

Do you know who you are? she asked

*In your dream? I asked*

No, who you are. At the river that day


*Yes, I said, but I wasn't there, then*

You were. You were my girl, my little girl

It was you pulled me upward

*I know, I said*

*Now I remember*

*It was my brother I pulled out, I said*
*We weren't supposed to be on the ice that day*

You almost drowned him, she said.
Your own brother, imagine.

*I saved him, I said*
*He froze so hard when I pulled him out*

He hadn't been born yet, she said

*You're thinking of your sister then, I said*, leaning into her hair,
the oil smell of the jacket & inner heat, the small ear & dwelling
& compulsion, the small branch of red flowers, the rose

it was you, she said

Spain begins at the Ebro

*That's a joke, I said*

Yes, she said

# The Splendour

Is it rigour or is it patchwork
Riding, alone, the engine of economy

A splendour
(or is it)

Trying to be as curious
Trying to forge an upset frame of reference
Pulling the window thru the door,
her blue sweater gradually emerges
or rocks where she had crossed

the Elbow River
A splendour (is it)
Following "Louise's" laugh
An economic dwelling where we all have been spilled or tarnished

Alone, but as such
I connote her arm where once no art was possible
A true life

we have been seeking
is it seekable

or "stake in"

2

What it is, we wait
as once we did
Await the father's anger which we knew as love
Tools & soil inhabit us

(it is so difficult not to be bitter
as such
Communicáte or icon, a slick rock she once did slip on
in the Colorado River, falling)

Because it is such difficulty names us . . .
I "admit"


3

A zone where tremors do inhabit
We are at ease here
Our heart shocks us every moment

A respite is what we long for
To be honest
I remain

4

Where keys of doors & doors of poetry
An insistent anecdote brings up her smile
Last seen in June (it is November)

As such, time passes
we refuse it
Kale, mimosa, milk & resin

Time passes
Poems recuperate, but do not solve
We refuse it

do not obey
or chastise

pulsate


5

The realm here is
irremediable

Thus in my act I do remember
what is memory
If not

aberrant splendour


6

I insist upon (falling into the fall or river, shoes wet)

to pulsate*

---

* imagine

# POURS, or What stills reveal about the human figure

We are beings inhabited by surprise.
When we are still, speech pours out of us.
There is a reason for our hair.

A reason reasons our hair.
Did a little mouse run around "here"?
Or were we truly innocent of tabulation.

When still we are not cadavers.
Our biographies are not synonymous &
not letdowns.

Always chooses a note, & fails to sedate it.
A particular grief is always "being" jettisoned
until the soil, a varnish, lets up.

Because I said so.
Because "located" in inhabited space.
Because arm, ar

Nos oublis sont là, visibles et non pas chimériques

C'est acceptable, on dit
D'où vient ce pain merveilleux, on dit

La question est posée derrière l'écran du corps
La question est serrée entre les doigts

du visible, d'où on vient, d'où vient
ce pain

ce

==================================
in a war, who lost an earlobe? who slept "right thru"?

## Two

Tomarric an invention of a yellow spice or trill
Her ear still says so, is still
Fabulous with innuendo

===============================================

in a war, who baked flageolets with lamb? who "furnished"?

## Three

There is an impetuous shadowing mirth
or Murph
-----------

His beautiful length of fur seen in stills only
Still exists in stills a concocted reverie
But mortal does establish this

A coin or "this"
We inhabit or are spending
Sloughs off the human figure or off the dog

We have not been able to say "dog" up till now
In any poetry
-----------

Si jamais on pouvait localiser la voix
Une corde de moins, l'empruntée ou "échec"
L'échouée

Today we are admitting certain consonants
as vowels
ovoid figures in a tested environment

Today we are admitting certain continents
as vow(el)s
Othered figurae in a viridial testament

====================================

in a war, who carried forward the plush moniker? who "wised up"?

# Four

Where we at last intended
a continent our gap still does disallow
my fortitude to admonish

As particular as any "new" regret
whose meaningful entity a swan song or landing
in a flecked home stilled

Our continent of admonish or disavow
The false dog who was no syllabus
but red hair & lopped or insistent grin

we cherished.
Some in him saw grey hound or razor cut above the eye
It was a catch-all

we did not inhabit
Car l'habitation implique la résonance de la mémoire
Car l'implication de la résonance écarterait la mémoire

Elle marche lentement vers ces pelouses vertes d'un hiver lointain
Pas habitable

=====================================
in a war, who wrung out the wet pyjama? who ached a stripe at noon?

# Five

If an ovation is a lesser form of "triumph"
She came out at last with a feature that wept
against terminology

or spire, spite, danger sputum
Too "is" has been a way this danger does inhabit
presently

we are "up for walks" upon the greening Mountain
which is to say a feature or designation
Proper to admit or ponder

Proper to concatenate or disinter
Where features project an original form of landscape
what we planted there in still

Heretofore "unavailable"
La comtesse qui boit du café à la lumière du jour
Ils ont écrit : la *précieuse* lumière du jour dans leur pays

=====================================
in a war, who came back with curtailment? who "pitched" an arm?

el: Firstly, there is a lot here for which to beg your pardon. The deer
came out of the hill trees to feed at the hot side of the building,
stalking drifts to get there. It means an awful slow motion over time
exposure. It was her house, there were still fallen apples. "Still"
admits to what duration? The palimpsest determines or deters me.
How will I know the answer, when I only *saw* the photos in which (&
this cannot be changed now) the lower half of her legs was erased by
the dog. A kind of pointing animal or reference out of the framework.
Aside from this, I only want to say: fervid, avid, fervorous, ardour.
These are the mechanisms I am trying to deal with. Yrs, er.

# 7 Cues to the Instability of Artistic Order

*for W., R., L.*

Oui j'irai à l'ambassade
pour te faire plaisir

prépare les valises
saute-moi bien

ou

autant de plaisir

Somnolente
somnolence
Écrasez-moi

je ne suis pas le pied de votre statue

ANECDOTE FOR W.

We are wearing our wooden receptacles
As if touching me could be short of honest

*By* me
Or touching
you by me
But that is

another way out of a dilemma

this dilemma
(the cat asleep on the "poem")

Yes I will go to the embassy
to give you pleasure

Pack the suitcases
Jump (over) me well

or

so much pleasure



Sleepy head
sleepiness
Knock me flat

I'm not the foot of your statue (yet)



ANECDOTE POUR W.

Nous portons nos réceptacles de bois
Comme si «me toucher» n'était pas assez honnête

*Par* moi
ou toucher
toi par moi
Mais ça c'est

un tout autre moyen de sortir d'un dilemme

ce dilemme
(le chat endormi sur «le poème»)

2

It took too many hours to come back
An image telephoned

Book book book

Fear is in the eye of my beholder

L'aveugle marchait à l'intérieur du poème
Qui a pris sa canne, et
comment

Le bois se termine enfin
« ici »

NARRATION FOR R.

Humus breeds a bitter soil, natural
She dwells wherein my fingers cherish
If such could now replace our fear

If such a dwelling, amicable
Your brown tress (short) &
azure gaze

Because the pages say so
You are ever welcome

Convocable, *chérie*

Tant d'heures pour y revenir
Une image a sonné

Livre  livre  livre

On ne voit bien qu'avec la peur


The blind one walked inside the poem
Who did take his cane, &
how

The wood is finally ended
"here"


NARRATION POUR R.

L'humus engendre un sol amer, naturel
Elle y demeure, là où mes doigts chérissent
Si cela pouvait remplacer notre peur

Si une telle demeure, amicale
Ta tresse brune (courte) et
ton regard d'azur

Car les pages le disent
Vous êtes toujours bienvenue

Convocable, *sweetie*

3

a)

We drew you up into its highest consequence

An abyss was where feeling wept, we were disgruntled surely

A particle separated from its core, is not an atom

We drew you up into the highest consequence


b)

If the poetic lineament is a finer line

A picture does, forever, always cherish

They say so is a redundancy that is, oneiric glee

If a poetic lineament is a finer line


c)

Je cherche tout simplement à vous abolir

my precious consequence

Naive a *may* we can discover

Je vous cherche simplement pour tout abolir

4

d)

If as such we are permissive beings

& ignore our consequence that does speak aloud *endure*

a trial ignominy dispenses juries' wanton membrane

If as such we are permissive ore


e)

A corpus agitates A concrete endeavour truly sings

or we are youthful can you imagine it

A C-note or bizarre

(is blurred)


f)

A body agitates A concrete endeavour tulip sings

5

Amen I called a shoulder to your ear
This a consequence does discover
Or amend

Thread of that sweater, I leaned on


Somnolence
somnolente
N'écrasez pas le poème

Je vous démontrerai toute mon affection
plus tard

Le jamais, jamais


STRATEGY FOR L.

The shorn-end of the mountain reach
seen from the lip of a *macchiato*
To ignore our consequence disperses
wisdome

A finger now I touch your countenance
By you or me

No one knows this

By you & me
To recognize

Amen j'ai appelé une épaule à ton oreille
Ceci une conséquence doit découvrir
Ou s'amender

Fil de ce chandail, je m'y suis penchée




Sleepiness
sleepyhead
Don't wreck the poem

I will show you all my affection
later

The never, never




STRATÉGIE POUR L.

Le flanc coupé de l'étendue montagneuse
vu de la lèvre d'un *macchiato*
Écarter notre conséquence disperse
la sagessse

Un doigt maintenant je touche tes lèvres
Par toi ou moi

Personne ne le sait

Par toi et moi
À reconnaître

# 6: The Usual Gratuitous Ref. to the V.

a)

To rise awhile our vein is *ainsi* freed

A sluice gate we have now traversed "let's go"

There is so much green    But image

But image    Turmeric awhile her vein is free


b)

A consequence does always us inure

or in habit, as in the artery's rope inside an arm

In written we have forged an orphic bond

Its consequence does always us inure


c)

Or speakable.

As we came in regular toil

Triumphant, a kind of light inside the thigh

Arc of this, speakable

7

Somnolence
Somnolente
Éclatez-bien la personne-poète
Éclatez-moi le poème

Je vous remercie
À tantôt




Sleepiness
Sleepyhead
Explode the person-poet well
Explode in me the poem

I give you thanks
Catch you later

# The Allure

*I have* not *stopped saying "if so"* E.M.

I

## A Reason for Lassitude

Things were messier than expected
There was a heart wound

Obedience was a fracture between two sides
of the drawn curtain

Complaisance entailment follicled a brocade

her whose a myrtle breast or condiment, allure
We wanted it to work out

We ached for it
to grow older

# A Fashion Précis

Life gets better before we notice
we have to believe we can obey

I see you hold the aspidistra
keep it flying
A small joy is not an inert quantity

to perceive merit, a learned profess
opposite to scoff

Fabulation observed in parents

I see you are wearing a new scarf now
May I call you Theresa with an h

The thespians are on alert there

## Dishing This

Trying to organize a paella did she blurt
*In esse* is a key to charm

Or whimsical a gesture she promulgates
to the letter

for disobey is to concatenate
Did we know this

When she turns I see the back clasp she coveted
from calypso

Oh

We have to believe we can compel
obedience's dictive flower

# Myrtle

Given weighed portions learned in "plating" classes
they snigger (they are "she"s)
Wanting to enact an important form

Alive our skin is valuable to the burned
The burned the burned the burned
A type of high art in a sentence, ruined
Tonal variants imply a verdant allure

We are mysterious falsettos or brides
our corridal "neve" in high snows

Foliate to amuse

They *felt us thru the feral membrane
all that time

2

## She's Answered It

Usually I find being distracting
do you agree

do you know if this is so

A tertiary fascicle stops in mid-track

tho you still will not admit
We separately believe what is necessary
or deem

now

Do our ideas fragment or coalesce
will we hold hands

Occasionally

(ever again,
oddly beaming)

# Cloves sans C

No one has given an answer to the proposed structure
Keepers

No, keepers absolve & we are waiting

Disturbances indicate grandeur of real life
is this a clue
or ministration

I am in need of ministration

A toil submit, will she
Why do I so fain or want her

A tall girl cracked me up, she admitted later

I have stopped saying "if so"

---

* "feared" cherished

# An abrasion Series

document1

(an abrasion serial)

(markings here)

)

document2

A grid accepts the weal of its interior energy

Particles of light descend now from the wall

Siempre tengo hambre en las mañanas.

A curative power is what she seeks, is not transcendent.

Mercy releases the synapses from the terrible
syllables of grief, which are "like"

the sky.

document2

A mediate foil the proscenium aggregates a scene

Her table beneath the welt collects a wealth of
particles*

Con queso.

As if ontology could be let to wonder & would not reach
beyond, to disobey.

Mercy portrayed in the dendrite of the human synapse,
lets go of
proper "memories", which invite

the $- - -$ .




document4

A tremulousness is what we cannot concatenate into
structure

A weal or caul in the system of capillary light

Nunca tengo miedo de la ventana abierta

A touch a consonant? She a woman she unknits is
being a shelter in

A coarsest etymology pretends a vigour
we cannot imply

or designate (my base desire or)

---

* prodigals

document7


(impertinence)
(abraded series)
(concupiscence)
(abraded series)

marmarmarmarmarmarmarmarmarmarmarmarmarmarmarmar

concatenate or disob
                    e y




document2

positionality detects a gravest wish to live

a series of invatical proscenity

because of immortal coil a sadness i do inure
& have said so to "her" gaze

positionality detects a gravest wish to live

positionality detects a gravest wish to live

positionaoty detects a gravest wish to live

# One response to a misquote from Wittgenstein

We are not at home anymore in our particles

A fendit does a vast bereave

Darkness a lamp can blur our varied speed
this is an agony singing this

A hot day in the chairs behind the building we did inhabit

Gaily forcing the trellis of arithmetic


2

Did you take calculus I did I liked this

Amneotic fluid of a caress or bewhilder

As it did me, I did not conceal

But did fend or moult or presentate a "wow"

Who spelled this, it's wrong at her


3

A cold kitchen is a true home will portend a scheme

Trace elements succeed where once we did defer

Eros was a cab we took a night too drunk for words

"A gas" the trees

Fecundate she cried out it was her hand, I knew

4

Impetuous gleam a roar begins anew a syllable

Her so delicate way we carefully did spell & not refuse

Her tender glance a fear or blitz

I did not conceal & wd not prevaricate

Obvious the conduit for communicative rendered it surprise
& must not cow a pharmakon


5

List as boats do

Going under

False pedestal

Aleph or coined

Positionauity

Faced to

"Apiary bees"*

---

* but no one answered the "pure signal", a sign for how it did sting me, how it did
truly sting

# Spills Her A Notes on Wit

A girl is kissing her new friend's smallest teeth
We are all such ratchet gestures
mortality behooves us

these practicalities
corruprt

search wit in wit's gloss or fêlure


❖

Wit intends wit's wry gesture

To stand up from the table laughing spills what concoct is then

a wit lights wit's innocence or peel

where wit's omphalos is wit's coiffeur


❖

What immajestical sentiment or faze
of resonant particules
"We meet" a least confabulation
her hair hope says
Learn hence for ancient rules
a just esteem
it gilds all objects but it halters none

from wit's impudence to wit's girl calor

❖

Search wit in germination
a the key inscribe her now
her bolten gossamer a least or veil to
enfoliate wit in wit's abeyancy
envigorate
or one veiled wit, her haunted night's attire

wit's perineum
where wit's indolence metes wit's gregare


❖

Memories of haunted
signals elucidate
Lips dwell where lips do dwell chérie
(honest)

Wit envious of wit's gay allure


❖

Unhappy wit's mistaken wing
atones not yet for fert amend

her judgement its fine calor
one glaring Chaos and wild heap this wit's

free from flattery or abrupt allure

Is wit's incipience at wit's grove?
but no, from this her crampèd hand
wit's scallawag hostess is wit's demeure

❖

Okay then the oatery's faint hill, not the
faine-hearted
Bitten hands are also "some coarse instruments"
Her gaze so shy in front of a soft lid node's abeyancy
Look away and let her, please
imagine
In wit's hearth, wit's bold artifice a fear
wit's scallawag is wit's demure

the her gorgeous crepusculum

❖

Wit's homely gest a coil of wit
where w. lives w. senses glee
It is amaze of wit's frilled pellicule

Fierce for the liberties of wit, and bold her bed

A soft call opens thought's permiss
wit's fascinate in that crevice is wit's procure
thought's ambience wit's lass,
thought's wit,

thought's trace a lure

wit's debit greeting wit's bravure

# Grief, or Sweetness for A.

*¡Qué no quiero verla!* F.G.L.

Was it a mistake in agony
Was it set in form

A mercurial handshake
Deleterious at that moment then

Then a

Having wrenched it upward & carried
The small stopped head

Flopped

Sideways

It is irreal or forgery
Is it irreal or _simply forged_
the panicked coves


ii

Is it a usual formal element
Synecdoche or in rhyme
Is it impervious to agony

A stopped head not palatable to eyes
A blood wound

A torn information in the fabricate of blood

then a

Is it a mistake in form
or formal dissonance
or form

iii .

An aural meticulousness
Craven
A respite is what we long for

The grasses lain down in the field, frozen white
From here we "see" it

(are told)

we are at ease here


iv

Who is running alone at night
a field or animate

All the light inside the stems of grain
Prefabricate or shut down in agony
The muscle of her chest a heart is
saying

"Will not
prevaricate"


v

The rail they dreamed of, a head's
torsional fecundity in the road

is it an irruptive method
is it a worn cut or tear in the neural organism

is the brain visible as an organ
not metonymic but as flowered

From here we are told

the small stopped head a wound that heals us
As if "simply forged" = beautiful⁰
in this articulation

Or wound

---

⁰ "tentative"

vi

But who we are
interrogates every consequence

(Berlin, Moscou, Hyderabad)

as if precedence demurs, *Elythea*
a fact of it

I lay yours there
It snowed at last


Sweetness is where we have lain it


-----------------------

*(a transit thru snow)

*Je suis un peintre.*

Christian Boltanski

*6.51 . . . For doubt can exist only where a question exists, a question only where an answer exists, and an answer only where something* can be said.

Ludwig Wittgenstein, *Tractatus Logico-Philosophicus*

*6.522 There are, indeed, things that cannot be put into words. They* make themselves manifest.

Ludwig Wittgenstein, *Tractatus Logico-Philosophicus*

*Je suis un peintre réaliste.*

Francis Bacon

*She dismissed the blind bird of narration.*

Barbara Guest *(misheard, misattributed)*

# The Her Sensorium

# Calor

*"Must our fear of sign-systems, and therefore, our investment in them, be still so immense that we search for these pure positions?"*
Jean-François Lyotard, *Libidinal Economy*

What is "set in motion"?
What "is cured"?
If so, "what is a remark"?
& what is justly "evident"?
Who "freaked out"?
Which woman "had a bird"?
Which held a blue teléfono *en el ruido de la calle*?
Who withstood hail?
Who watched at the moorish embellishment of stone?
Which one ordered the 3rd bottle between 2 on c/ Elvira?

Whose reason "stank"?
Whose version was missing a forehead?
"Who is Andalusian"?
Who "stuck her neck out"?
Who, because?
Who "felt grief"?
Whose heart was a "cherish, aimless girl"?

For whom did the name "cohabitate"?
Lying in the narrow room over the cut wood.
For whose heart, grazing her shoulder?
For whose light jaw, its touch of grain on that tangled shoulder?

Where faith was?
Where the odious was a syllable?

Who painted.
Whose fear tore out, leaving the gauze.
Whose veil vanquished.
Whose furious gaze bore no answer?
Who shuddered in such, "in such" a wind?
Whose "wound" bore cause?
Whose syllable met "who"?

I love you. A use? Te quiero.
Whose "was" the Atlantic storm? Who brought rain?
Who did we "ever know" "enough" of?
Whose crater vanquished?
Whose "seemed"?

Whose arroyo winked its pellicule?
Who was there at noon, holding the fresh gauze
on the plaza where the rain spattered
on the book with the cloth-bound cover
on the cobble where the cortical gruel of the accident
                    finally vanished

Because it rained
Because its gutter was a Tuesday's worn endeavour
A microchromatica of the blood
A treasure of sane belongings
An object of doubt . . .

Whose tome fenestrated daylight?
Whose wore, for awhile, a rough sheen?
Whose surface was "calm"?
A horse intruded.
Whose declaration "mattered"?
A gate of doors.
Whose dream vanished?
Whose dream stuttered an achey name?
A dog intruded.
A calm.

An absolute sonorousness
sinew of her shoulder.
Jerks in sleeping.
Sinew the noise of water, a fountain at dusk lit up
Confabulate "a body" enter.
Fain.

(Not a gate or horizon.
Not a cleft we have known.
Not a "spirited girl". This she was lent only for a moment. This
she borrowed. This a swank gauze she could not honour or
defend. This a sorrow's touch of so much "human feeling".
This the name of water out of "some" fountains. This a
sentence containing "those blousy men". This a fragrance of
lent oranges. Her shoulder. This


her shoulder? Her shoulder. A leaning, *con su permiso*. That once.
It was set in motion. No one of us had eleven. No "once" of
us was cured.)




THE COLD

There was a cold
In which

A line of water across the chest risen
(dream)

Impetuate, or
Impetuates

Orthograph you cherish, a hand her
Of doubt importance

Her imbroglio the winnowing of ever
Does establish

An imbroglio, ever
she does repeatedly declare

to no cold end
Admonish wit, at wit's end, where "wit" is

❖

The cold of which
her azul gaze impart a stuttered pool

Memoria address me here (green)

Echolalic fear
Her arm or name in French says "smooth"

A wine-dark seam inside the head, this name
The "my" head I admit, or consonantal glimmer

Insoluble
Or wet fields the vines or eucalyptus wood

Lift from, here


Whose cartilage did grief still bear?
Whose silent wound?
Who submitted?
Who fortuitously was grave?
A trepidation honest
Whose declaration met silence?
Whose demurred?
Whose wall shored up became
houses?
Whose "will"?

Whose sympathetic concatenation? Whose picture
withstood "ordeal"?
Who caressed "that tiger"?
Whose laugh at an airport called forth? Whose ground
shifted?

# THE EXTIRPATION

A train of cold
Obviates

The sheer endeavour it does exclaim
is not the "end" of "hope"

(But who heard "rope" here?)
or circumstance

An inattendant way of looking
(hers)

whom doubt forfends
attentive to longing & circumstance

mine
not easeful yet

attentive to doubt or circumstance

her claim for
A consequence

weight of

Otherwise, what light was it?
Otherwise it was a far-off home "that told that"
Who "fouled up"?
Who treasured days of "scampish" glee?

Whose sobriety wakened?
Who toiled thru?
Whose immense shoulder populated so softly a place for her?
Who cherished the impossibility of place? Who said *sursum corda*?
Who did so?
Who murmured pax vobiscum?

Whose stylus composed in dread?
For whom the "first scene" did always flutter?
Who recuperates a seed's endeavour?
Whose "speak" does a ventricle entail?
At whose insistence, "punto", was the boat-wire torn?
Who trembled at this crossing?

Who turned back?

Whose conversation at great distance was comical, "hello"?
Whose continents were tectonically cathected?
Who availed her scribe of such cathects?
Who pleased?

Did she turn back?
Did this one uncross the two wands of the foregone?
Was her armistice weak from so much audible stone?

But whose breath caught "just there" on the seam?
Whose collegial honour?
Whose echo of indigenous mirth?

Which one's savagery mended an internal sigh?
Whose was graced?
Whose avenue open to a fold of rain?
Who quaked, for the first time, reaching such
an avenue?
& whose shudder turned back?
Whose horse cherished?

Who sang her moult filament into the pale pulsion of the skin?

Who was judged?
Whose mirth was judged, thinking it "mettle"?
Who "carried it off"?
Whose sleeve brought a protocol?

& whose item abolished?
Who annihilates? Who cleaves?
Whose finite terminaison was carried out on two spindles,
a virxen to the romería?
Whose phantasm brought glee?
Whose base offer?
Whose garment, of whose ear?

Whose voice? Whose claim, belated, sufficed as "joy"?

(Here we talk about a telephone, a simulacrum of her voice, heard
at such a distance. The word "cuerpo" is a direction or source
that cannot be conveyed by the word we have here, "body". The
"cuerpo" can receive its benediction or veneration from any
person or girl. "Here" too far for gesture to contemplate. The
relation of the "cuerpo" to wet herbs, the two kinds of thyme
on the hill where I stood above the Fuente Grande. "I"? (Mirth.)
A simulacrum of narration. The page is not an interpretative
conjunct but cellulose. Oblative. What gesture "is". Or jest.* )

---

* In this way we thought to get rid of footnotes, those calamities. But
why are you still wanting to kiss her? Once again, a wise fold or figure
does carefully allude. Ardent is "disobey".

Why was the seam torn?
In the soft garment of women
In winter, such cold, why was the seam torn?

THE COLD

An extirpation is her way to marvel
Doubt's tremor

& names us
(its valve)

a small beauty does perfectly endure
in memory

without regard to hope or fear
this treed company

a figure

almost (opening a Valdepeñal window, seamless
also a door

Whose aureole glistened, after?
Whose laid down an arm, so gladly?
Whose surprise incorporated?
Whose clavicle held a soft murmur outward?
Whose sternum was alabaster in relief?
Whose sun warmed it, such a sternum, in such, "in such" a key?

Who said "such" as if the heteroclitic band would glisten?
Whose head "spun"?

Who traced that aureole with a lip or femur?
Whose turned back?

(Here we are talking about the voice, a simulacrum of the *cuerpo*.
Who dressed "consequence" in such gaudy shoes? Whose
blessing was obvious, a limen? The word "cuerpo" is already
the repository of such a distance, & bears the topological trope
of rhetoric. Where we were going in the narration. The body
admits to this, a kind of precocious tear or tear, a narrational
knot it feeds. & if Lyotard says he will speak no more of
"surfaces of inscription", it will be necessary to undo his
interdiction. The surface of inscription not a place but a danger.
A line is foraged there. Abrasion hears us where a line is.)

Whose aureole?

(An inscription insists, insists.)

Whose mouth says "aureole"?
Whose transcription, urgent, hears what the mouth says?*

---

* Oh who says the mouth says anything. The mouth, tongue, convex
& concave surfaces of the membranal capacitator, able to invest "cooking".
Attached to the organs of digestion, & for that matter, to the lungs &
respiratory organs. The lungs. A surface 25 times greater than the skin,
folded. 500 million doorways directly into the blood.

All this is the blood then. A dark vigour. A passage. But whose sobriety
wakened? Who pressed through?

# THE CHORD

Courageous lair "might prevail"
Waking up to her your "yellow coal"

Steals a its way

harm's imbrogliatic murmur
to concatenate

has been "said"
a mortal habitation or cut in air

that air leaks through

here too


❖

Tricked again out of
hope's chord

The oscillatory hum in the head, or
amygdala

continual reaction in the wet mouth to
old oranges, or

mistakes* in form
"I retain a clear memory of afternoon light".

A vertebra unfolds its wing, its smallest
wing, the pleasure particulate of such a wing

(harp's corde)

a our mycelium

---

\* regrets

## THE COLD

If she administers her own abject moral
enhancing the recorded indice of the foregone

green light of fearful "might" be leaves
Who ate "what"

my signature connives a doubling fear

signet wary

ser   her


❖

Mezclan  ical  ho  tir
flon  e  irreg  obot  kre  ot

her green-blue haze


## HER INSCRIPTION

d b r

l r

h z l

synaesthesia, where "sweetness" the
expression or vesicle of grief

*Une perturbation du monde par le corps*

Whose gesture forbade lament?
Whose "came clean"?
Who precipitated?
Which countenance repaired mirth?
Which held a cancer upward in a doorway?

Who cherished.
Whose method bore fruit?
Whose piety betrayed a laugh.
Whose configuration was droll in the afternoon?
Whose vast antelope died from bread?

Who marvelled?
Who "stewed"?
Who was her own "worst enigma"?
Whose feature was an implicit groin?
Whose capability danced & "up & down"?

Does nature conceal the fragment of the skin
felt suddenly before braking?
Does a wheeze medicate for all that is absent?
Does a clavicle inhibit, or permit?
Is the strange cast to the doorway "matter"?
Is there a pentiment of gloom?
Does the horse's bird follicle change his a quarters?

If swank seductiveness incarcerates daylight
in a seam?
Orb?
A collectivity finally matters or desists
A torn shudder inebriates daylight
The forms,
The punctuated,
The physical tremolo in the vagina,
The comma in the departed tune,
The photograph of Federico *cerca la fuente*,
The press kit of Annette Funicello, the representative of *duende*,
the focal point where they "plunged in"

If they did so

A commemoration inhabits
A commemoration to refute the thin match of nostalgia
Por que no puede contestar sus preguntas
A commemoration of salience inhabits this prose

Features are timely endeavour
A proscenium tart unveils a wanton scene
Who called her forth from the a reign of silence?

Who transmitted infinite carbon?
Who amassed perturbations in the chest?
Whose labial tendency still is warm?
Whose traumatism succeeds, in augmenting the
nervous coin brought from childhood?
Whose fortuity remembered thyme?
Which syllable brought an abeyance to "here"?

Whose bliss rescinded?
Whose was brought to Spain? Spain, that inner *Spain*,
España,
that last arroyo, that pellicule, that oration of a pen . . .

What mood?
What sign?
What thin trail of obedience passed for "love"?
The thin wedge? A trespass?
Corpus callosum?
The cut in the side of bread?

Who was implacable?
Who was faced with glee?
Whose cord of hope resuscitated its her flame?
¿Quién se llama "nada más"?
¿Quién espera?
Who swayed blindly, under the lottery tickets outside
the Dakar?
We all have ankles.
Whose chair shed tears?
Who navigated the sill between two pale cheekbones?
Whose kiss was "not" pure?

Whose silence "feigned"?

# THE COLD

Living as we are
beneath the wet shelf of a "penal code"

we forget a
sunlight on orange paint, a stucco wall

is ever more synonymous
with the etched caprice of human feeling

herself foreborn
Is there a word for "this" but "this"

If there was, would it be
Kapuskasing when we were young, unknowing

bearing the weight of fathers
a few leaves, leopards, sole impediments


❖


Sometimes a blue light
before traffic

scolds us & Sue too

Plural or established
Inveterate

The cold precedes & contains "me"
"her"

"wise cattle" "humans" "dogs"
lakes of water, trees, sesame, arugula




Whose bestial worry came across as sound?
Who was imperiously "calm"?
Whose feature smudged?
Whose cauldron left room for grief?
Whose habitable longing?
Who charged forth, smitten? An angle of "this"

Whose interest provoked a doorway?
Who, unknowingly, strolled through?
Whose castigatory membrane, then, vanished?
For a moment or day, vanished & freed her?

Whose tolerance confronted a wanton veil?
Who misheard the word as "dove"?
Whose treatment of chrome?

An end to anxiety or leaves a lustre
The face "seems" to inhabit
Who would prefer "established charms"?
Whose harsh portrayal? As prodigal or amused?

Who knew?
Who bore forward the "risk of voluptuousness"?
The risk "of figures"?
Whose insistence on the unfinished infinite portrayal of the foregone?

(Or who invented this risk to get out of a bad situation.
Generations of snow fell on the plains between them, & on the
jackets of the forebears, the sheets they wore pulled over their
tricornes & bandanas in the high sierra, just behind "Ontario".
If so, whose invention was honest? Who stopped potentizing a
cure? Who gambled away "god's mouth" on two tickets? If
only the snow had frozen those forebears, we wouldn't be in
this base conundrum.)

THE DILATION

Where habit's preponderance is dilation

Or delight

Doubt's tremor exists us,
pares our boundary

to flatten the precocity of "mean"
to be trepanned

❖

Who fouls up? Whose mad glee?
A purpose?

Impetuous gleam is too
a treatment of scorn

or scorn's imbroglio
which is, at last, "délice"

or to possess a deepened feeling

you can see the trail of haste has left us

our figura, weal

What is "an act"?
What is "in front of"?
What is corpus spiritus mundi?
Mundum exemplar?
What is a curve or sheen?
Whose semicircular endeavour?
Whose protuberance bore a spatial veneer?
Whose last?
Whose perfect orb rendered a foot "wise"?
Whose astonished?

Whose hand wedded an obstruction in time?
Whose weight polished a quest where she was seen?
Who wore "trespass" to a forge?
Whose phosphorus bore a sign of doubt?
Whose tongue melded? Who felt the tongue enter?
Whose foil?

Who saw space as a "terrible deed"?
Whose wound "accomplished"?
Whose compositional program resulted in "Anon"?
Whose resulted in infatuation?

Whose photograph was not sent?
Which intermittent sequel mattered?
Which one had the torn sail?
Whose emblem was composited in stone?

Before a wonder her arm climbing in that frenetic wood, above
an ocean, impetuous the valenced trait I cannot forego or
conceal, playing out the tasks of ardour in that inner Spain, my
most sincere reversal, a curious grain of light or hurt releasing
pulses. This &, repeatedly, her tremendum.)

This &, repeatedly, her tremendum.
An act of which, bestows or

thrives. Or
thrives.

I love you. A use? Te quiero.
Whose "was" the Atlantic storm? Whose brought "rain"?
Who was "unwieldy" in a marble caryatid of grieve?
Who caused "fanfare" at the sound of?
Whose spinal mendacity "chilled out"?
Whose muscle turned into a terrible cord under the skin?
Who said "girl of steel", meaning the lungs?

Who did we "ever know" enough of?

Whose crater vanquished?
Whose canalisation immodeste?

Whose silence "rained"?




THE COLD

Inequal light permits a cold
fenestration

wherein our particulars vanish or
assume

Horticulture becomes a way
out of "figurative" light

a doorway

Albeit our cherished feeling
has not been removed

By the lines' caught
tonsure of debt & circumstance

A hand, for "caress" establish

Immutably vigilant
"queer"

Which crenellated forehead?
Which intaglio of a "step" foreblown?
Whose simulacra quenched a bitten nerve?
Whose prospered?
Whose spectral anguish meant a "potato" was "fried"?
Who adopted nation to the word "house"?
Who said "a Serb house"?
Which one was "paltry"?
Which one did not respond?

Whose fortuitous gethsemane seeded toil nights of girlish joy?
Whose "wormed in"?
Whose was dilatory in front of a curled hand?
Who smoked or smouldered?
Who lay hers down?

Whose touch on "whose" fingers first intimated?
"Felestial" was "celestial" spelled wrong?
Abraded insignia fell from which shoulder
How prevail, or prevalent, were the signs?
"To be" in the word "ser"?
To question the compartment where grief wore up
its cinder?
To touch a breast to such a cinder?
Praetorian glean?
To beatitudinally correct a line?

To wit, where "wit's end" was?

(Her laugh could continue in the head or repeat a tape-looped
image or motor. But at that same moment she was silent. At the
same moment her urge was already gone. There were other
modes of doubt or blazons. The stone woman in the slot at the
gothic wall, her gaze. But whose syllable? Whose fondness, bred
in the fingers? Whose troubled "air" or "haze"?)

Who worked with the "smallest window" of "hope"?
Whose bandage liquored a her sigh?
Whose fell?
Whose interminable phrase wandered?
Which one "held her breath"?
Which one's breath "held"?
Which one felt "the thickness of paint"?
Some of it was cadmium, that toxin, that
"most beautiful of metals".
Some of it was a smear of red to delineate the visible
behind her jaw?
Some of it was abraded from the room's light

If so, where does a question establish?
Is a grammar also a "bonyness"?
Is there a hybrid correlative for "life"?
Is the timbre on the inside of her thigh audible?
Does audibility leave a mark?
Is this mark "cherished"?
Is there a way to "respond to a sentence as a Roman"?
We are absolved or astonish?
If we astonish?
If a clue hears its symptom of a "wet aorta"?
If a crevasse gives up its mortal lake?
If a "three trees" can be found where she
waited & read Rousseau?
There is an article to absolve grief?
There is a plume?
There is a vanishment a bestowal?
A pentiment of a hock or knee?
A swivel symptom throughout, the description of
a neck?
A phrase who collapses, a patient wearing
the nightgown to an operation?
Its prell?

A silence (her laughter) cohabiting with this prell?
Touch her ear or syllable?
Prevent or disinfer?

(If another one would have called them at that very moment, the
thirst slaked from a jar. A foil astonishes, the gleam of a wet thigh
where a line was drawn from the head's lip, the lip of the other,
a girl. To astonish a herborium. To bring forth doubt is also to
"cherish". "Do the solitudes feel?" Do these prescient confluxes
confer, or found? -------------------------------------------
------------------------------------------------------------
-------------------------------------)


Who "rose up"?
Who penetrated a firmament of glee?
Whose fixture brought joy to a soft hand?
Whose eye sought where sought was?
Which this was "this" known?
Which parenthesis drawn round "doubt"?
A perpetration of a fleet moment?
A taboo withdrawn into caress?
An aimless girl's sentiment to cherish?
A particle of uplifted gloom?
A sated note in the bowl or socket of wet bone?

Could we be prefigured in such a syllable?
Could our philosopher's garment render doubt?
Could circumstance fain the nougat of ardour?
Could "exist" tremble in the groin?

Who registered an oration of doubt?
Whose pulse convected a praetorial arrangement?
Whose love read "luck", there, or in
the Upanishads?
Whose broke down?
Who "coiled a learnt rope"?
Who "braved" impediment?
Who called out "ojo por ojo"?
Whose breast ached at the very left where touched "once"?
Who wrote "último", or "trajectory", thereafter?

What crescent learned grief in a road?
Whose dog's eyes stared "up"?
Whose vigil mattered? A missing "r"?
Who called out, the imperturbable?

Whose light fixed on an her ear?
Who, seeing this ear, gradually, came to shore?
Who came to shore?
Who, seeing it, gradually came to shore?

Obedience here was a brave lectern. Here was a page where grief had
been cemented. The arbours grew space for these two girls. The arbours
"came" to them. This was their arbour.

Who remembers, "doubt was banished".
Was doubt banished?

Was there another, another name?

If the complication's ragged note of salience?
Do the solitudes amass or "feel"?
Is a drubbed key a particular of the her sternum?
Do we medicate for doubt?
Is circumstance a metography in the ear?
Her seasonable embellish?
Her way with a trout?

Her obvious grip to the palatable signet?
A wariness or "to fend"?
That bend in the armature of circumstance?
An oboe with a red fruit?
The full note played by a cancer?
A pusicle of immended glout? Abended? Hoyne?


## THE COLD

Bewitch a scar of her a groin
establish mirth here

o speak to me of girls, girls, girls
is inappropriate

to confer belief
A wine or faint glow circumstance

her an endeavour to ignite
these capable priestesses

Aron a heightened touch or weal
be to plague (placate) my labial curl

doubled or entwined
caesural

But if impetuous hailed.
Topically hailed.
If she, lips of. Wanting tectonic instrumentality or phase?

Who wants such, such a heated gaze?
Who said it without dread?
Who anchored?
Whose "love" anchored? Who said "here"?

A testament. A filamental surge.
Whose sobriety weakened?
Who toiled through?


## THE COLD

A cold of what could fail
or trek

But can we speak or mitigate a
failure here

A broached circumstance to endure
her arm bent "usually"

confers
Establishment a nougat

ardour did thus visitate
"made" or harkened

vocable a word's tentation
coalescent

for vocabular trees

her a rapture of, enrapt
entry of groin's syllable

Which one's rictus "came" in etymolic pleasure?
Which merited or endowed?
Who permits?
Whose rector of emphatic stone?
Whose figura deduction is a coloratura?
Creatine of the lung?
A "narrow miss" we cohabit?

Whose chiasmatic imbrication of the visible?
Whose subtle broach of "dear"?
Who feinted?
Whose tome glistened "*hors le texte*"?
Was her textual endeavour a mortal glean?
Was its topography craven?
Were there eggs or stars?
In the wound where the light fell, a swordsman?
Is there an accountancy that marries the rock of grief?
How so?

Forensic?
A few payments for a "plough" in tonic soil?
Her wayward fenicule?

Whose indurated habit?
Whose rictus of the phrase brought a her motivation to a grove?
Which one had the hearing of a diode teacup?
Which one, picking the bloom, made leaves treble?
Which haptic gleam portrayed a patina on the thread of solace?
Which one's wanton call, consequent?

Who located?
Who "poured forth"?
Whose abstemious nature was curtailed?
A momentary lapsus, curtailed . . .

A figural stutter in the mondial "dear"
A fesicule immortalized in the lineament of "dross"
Of a cartographer's mint correction

If we "set forth" sooner?
If our arm bands of the hospital murmured less?
If the capistus hazily draught amend?

Who says the spictal quantity must prevail?
Who calls forth the modicum?
Whose line has "wandered"?

## IT IS A LIFE

If between us there could be
no cold

What abscess would permit
assail

The marker we have each "set" out
in federal calm

Glistens

A harbour quintessent each of us
will shun

where "will" is a lip's brent impediment
an inner scoff

a difficulty
a pure difficulty of designate plume

though to say "so", makes us laugh
seismic in figuration

wrenching, again, the cord of believability
we turn from

each day
waking into the a salt

What is "a fact"?
What is the alterity of the visiple?
What is "in favour"?
What is "a sentiment"?
Who calls forth "miasmic plurality"?
Who wishes for "something else"?
Who craves "human feeling"?
Who "remembers" such an act?

Could the peripheral act vanish?
Could a typography coagulate to permit?
Whose altercation the reconnaissance of childhood?
The birth of the father?
All daughters' witness? Amass or perturb?
Juncture or this dress?

Whose plasticity in the advent bore a wound?
Who appealed to "corporeal resonance"?
Whose opacity was a "thickness" in the letter,
a coin awry?
Whose elemental thickness "took its toll"?
Which one "told" forth?
Whose metamorphal designation?
Whose spiritus of an arm forewarned?
A haptic elekance?
The risk borne onward, "those voluptuous bodies" . . .

Does corporeality bereave?
Is there a rictus ordained to the a syllable?
Is a syllable's accountancy a mnemonic for a vagina in "release"?
Does corporeality beaticate a shadow to the page?
Attend fixedly to small pressions?
Torsion of a geeky doubt?
Flaunting her aureole as a particular?

# THE INTEGNUM

Image a wordy trait
establish

the cold to
profligate an insecure

A "deepened feeling" or weal
no circumstance can designate

her a patinal phrase astonish "me"
Before that perfervid letter

her arm's insistinence extends
a small plate or scriven seal

fish with yellow
sauce & corn, to designate

"Imagine"

"hacking through"
those went particularities



Whose obus was syntagmatically displaced?
Whose feature evoked a paralogicall quintesse?
Which narrativity was constitutive of a breach in time?

Whose anamorphatic investissement of a bloom?
Whose labial composite shed the notoriety of dread?
Whose syntagmata are visible on a hand
after an incident at her forge?
Which girlish hands forgot? It is not possible . . .

Who abstracted an armature from a temporal duration?
Whose snatch of a melody of joy?
Whose beheld "figural destiny"?

Whose comparison harkened?
If the answer was female?
Whose Vesuvius wore a brigade to an answer?
Was a trip to the chair of Cassiopeia? Cylindric? To a
star?

Who, in the peripheral membrane, "sees"?
Who, in the peripheral corticule, "sees a dog"?
What is "haunting the ext"?
What "cherish"?
What "inure" or simply "give"?

(To desire a moot or mouth, an explanatory vigour of her
wanders who does confect inures a delicate membranality of
"sweet life".)

(-----------------------------------------------------------
------------------------------------------ rapt ----------------
------------.)

(But to confect is to disinter, a glimpse of so much "human
feeling", its her neural pull localized in the chest, a powder
immune to or sanctifying wonder, the wondrous, "this" image
of a room she now leans in, toward small leaves, a door, the
table. The place where she let fall the petals. That neurography
of a street or coin. That spelt conject.)

(Is there a this but this?)

(Does corporeality bereave or permit?)

(Intraceable?)

(What coalescence of a wisteria revealt?)

Which haze a mandible she embraced at noon?
Her funicular?

Her retimence in an orb?
Her orb?

The ever?

# THE EXTIRPATION

The signet now
"goes mad"

A childhood aim this spring
uncoils

Permits a haptic trough or irrigate
a seam permit

To counteract a cold
there is

To immediate a harsh life
Richly

Immediate
A heat to

"Their rays shook outward"
"Streaming"

"Invent"




Which one described "the nature of a– t"?
Which historic encrustation?
Whose "determinant ground" was judged "avail"?
Or prosecute a claim to disinfer?
Arbour with a "d" in wit?
Amitiographically permitt?
Eschew?

Fandango. Inebriate fandango. Implacable a her tarentelle.

Whose timorium valenced a geeky name?
Whose fent majuscule of a "cooked goose"?
Which one's integument called forth, impetually?
Quare non hac hora finis turpitudinis meae?
Atlantic for a trained deer?
Sobre todos.
Who went forth?
Whose rent garment follied a fenum pleure?
An insufflation to a doubt?
The "her" sensorium?
Amend? Her this?

# The Wittgenstein Letters to Mel Gibson's Braveheart (Skirting her a subject) (or *girls girls girls*)

*"offered, it was a gift"*

## (You place)

With you an immediacy stalls
forget
An impediment erases eons of its prate existence
A portion of grief is also forestalled
*as liquid entry*
placed (you place) into my syllable
Into the flow dichotomy of my forestalled
syllable
A face in the node of presence (you place)
your hand's heart in a gloved immediacy
*played out*
as blur or ectomic splendour
wherein (you place) your eyes' wench or girlish
affligency, profligate version, your version
my hand obeys to open into rough & "brave
immediacy", our hope where hope found
not foundered

found

A brave light in a world where obey
is its infernal mechanism
a ghoul or snow whose want of life perpetuates
an unspeakable

*But you*
in your hands obey is my lock to open
dressing silver upon a spent anatomy
to weigh my world against your fond persist
what you attach to name me
your arms or (you place) it is a presence

Impels immediacy
Stalls "forget" into a reign of thunder
To be with you
Amaze a frillt pellicule
Lust a frillt sustenance*

---

\*    *go ahead do it babe squirt yr babe-juice in my eye*

## (Their tautology)

If two sides of "therefore" are a mete descend
An argument connoting west particulars
A nativity arrangement wherein your injection permits
my fertile quantity
Your pull above my average

where content is a moot commodity
& substance the form a kiss entreats
before it brings on the majesty fourfold
of its pretend

which is not pretend
but of an utter quantity, which is bravery's course
in a mine of days in a universe of signs
"absolutely"
the throat he wore to say this in the burned movie
from his own throat trembling you have cited to me

& I want to be rigged in your frail coast of imperative ambition
Call forth from me my unknown tress of real dignity

Immortality in libraries

# (Her glad hand)

❖❖❖

"What is questionable in the production of a text, its evidence
and the history of all experience"

"The piano disappeared or there had never been a glad hand
equal to your structure"


❖❖❖

Which is not "pretend" but "allow"
which is & has its febrile quality
the febrility I say to you of which "its quality"
transgress a mere
confectability
a histoire of trust abeyed in an orifice
an offering unconditional of such an orifice

your spurt or burst into my dwelling
where I do not admit the grail
of culpability & you do not bring it to me

I am that pure my stake is to belie intransigence
in its very nature
your mouth where my breast will be astounded
now, collating the breadth of your lungs' consequence
if I say where your foot lay today* at my insistence
invokes a bestial restive repagination
a cathect of lidded nodes & soft
you would not eradicate
but use
not eradicate but incite
not eradicate but bless
but insist upon
but answer with your tautest femur
with your amaze of breast & insistent femur
beneficent to
employ   defend   enamour   tress


*28 January 1997, 2pm, The Lakeview

❖❖❖

*Ludwig:* "My propositions serve as elucidations in the following way: anyone who understands me eventually recognizes them as nonsensical, when he has used them – as steps – to climb up beyond them. (He must, so to speak, throw away the ladder after he has climbed up it.)"

*Norma:* "The way we have always been given to them, and so, focusing on them, affecting transparency, one narrates. One falls through the rungs of the ladder."

❖❖❖

## (A girl profligacy)

"The talk we could have
in the furnace of our differences"

"In that place facticity impairs us"

"we are agog across our boundaries,
agog not reactive"

"it is ever a febrile quality"

"quand arriveras-tu dans mon jardin peuplé
de consonnes"

"quand me libéreras-tu dans mon jardin peuplé
de mes propres auréoles"

"she treasured my intractability & told me
not to explode in the tricastin
of her caress"

"& I did, what wound I had made available"

"& she was intractable in my caress"

"& did not abjure me, did

not affront, did not deny, or

"abjure"

❖❖❖

If a substance could bear regret

An egret flag oh Marie our rooftop calliope flew

We did our homework (ajar)

You supposed that cuff could hold me
(tienes razón)

I appeased you? You appeased me?
A construction of *that* boundary did not happen.
It was a world rather
where neither of us acquiesced, but presented.

At last we determined "it".
*Either* you said: "You wanted to do *that* to me for quite awhile,
didn't you" *or* you said: "I wanted you to do *that* to me for
quite awhile". In any case, a smart remark, &
you pushed your head onto my palm in the moving vehicle.
Your coltishness a first dance.
Your first dance.
Your spigot.
*Your red boy.*


❖❖❖

N: "We were travelling together at speed. I saw or 'felt' my friend
go on. At speed. At speed I crashed full into a wall.
. . .
What is the inscription without a reader?"

L: "When something falls under a formal concept as one of its objects,
this cannot be expressed by means of a proposition. Instead it is shown
in the very sign for this object."


❖❖❖

# (Whose adoration)

Whose wing impersonates a wing or crutch, whose flight
arrest is her a syllable, a syllable administered
as caress or
endeavour, an almost insistence I show you in my
centre being,
arose or venerate, which you venerate or
venerate by fuelling, by utter portrayal, by the instance
of your body's choice & the wield
imparts me,
imparts my wrist or hip
*to feel the grace of such impediment*
or grace

to be adorned by you & this your pediment
to permit your wiles to cathect insertion
to coil my wrist where I have lived después de la intervención,
the wrist of bluest wine the IV did enter, the
light removed to permit your utterance
of a chosen syllable, of a length you chose to occupy or dwell me,
to cathect a demeter of torn profligacy, or warm & lidded
node display
& trust a prescient being & space torn instrument outward
& & trust your use of space pulled upward
& & & be your trusted use & obligation

your feature of west experience*

---

\*   *mess me up babe w. your hand coiled round & thumb turned in permits an entry*

# (Tremendous assertion)

Oh force of your insistent pellicule

Appetite to fuck (why not just out & say it)

Impresentientally, an ouverture or opening

Cantankerous was a word you told me for
your abandoned feeling

A trip or lure across a boundaries

A moult hair upon the lip to wander

O caress me, fond *jerk*, fond *insolence*

Ablate a tendency

Fornicate as the past tense of its own verb, or an
adverbial tag as in, when she pulled her girlish wield from me
I looked so fornicate

Your mouth went soft "then" she advised in splendour

Odalisk

Multiplicate

Abey

❖❖❖

L: "Roughly speaking, to say of *two* things that they are identical is nonsense, and to say of *one* thing that it is identical with itself is to say nothing at all."

N: "difference lies in constraints"

L: ". . . We can foresee only what we ourselves construct."

N: "At first it seemed additive then holds back, not necessarily narrative but told"

❖❖❖

A prolected trail        beatitude

                       wanting

                       want

                       beatitude

a facticity your pleasure does itself convey
holding a her marrow still, as if
my wrist inverted amnesia early on
*(how you knew this)*

& was still cohabited
your hard coil break around my aimless fact to dwell
my accent snared in your wet emphatic turn
"Happily" was not my word till you abolished "told"
& I took you there to where a corridor "as if"

& we abolished

The parade of wan thunders speaking from your
core

Indigenous

*fescue*

## (Bestows profound benefits on her practitioner)

Febrile is my fendish fent my practice spent in
all my entity
my wettest furl against your taut anatomy keels such a wrap-like frieze
incursion into my swain library

her my shudder abends us both
or *each a girl*
a her transects a quelled imperial quality
to "collect" my thought your lip the femur snares anew

your origin a wet wreck shirt where you had touched me
to convey a wield yr wrist's deft quantity alloys my fond allure
to convey an object benefit

(rend)*


❖❖❖

L: "Objects contain the possibility of all situations."

N: "The object is always waiting. How

    do we know what makes it

    visible: the object is waiting

       the object is visible

       waiting is visible"

L: "Objects are just what constitute this unalterable form."


❖❖❖

*your cheek fierce thrust its opening back upon my leg to raise*
*a cry out splendour is*
*held ajar*
*visible is waiting*

---

\*     *your concoct avail upon my leg to concatenate, streaming out yr liquored whorl a cry*

## (Socially-constituted objects include ourselves)

If "oh" knows us, dear ache of windward time
distance my heart absolves its propitious wane a bliss
to confess or herein
abjure an abject frame

we exist our skins a pellicule against that loss
an intent or admission "cares"

Our eyes, opened
cannot be shut now (time is big)
what memory falsifies in fact
A glance or
breath restores

a desert we dreamed of & did not abjure the dream

Comments are
bigger

prolepsis' antiquity is far your lovely harshness meant for me
your hand admits my interpretation, grandeur of water

her noise is


bent upon the serial productive whore of imagination

❖❖❖

*L*: "The truth-conditions of a proposition determine the range that it leaves open to the facts. . . . A tautology leaves open to reality the whole– the infinite whole– of logical space:"

*L*: "But in fact all the propositions of logic say the same thing, to wit nothing."

*N*: "It's very simple. They open the floodgates and water pours
    down at a fantastic rate of speed and with tremendous force,
    smashing you against the rail.

    Something with will is called into play."


❖❖❖

confess a momentous quantity

juts her a rift in time

"to her" I want to shake her by the hand

my insertion overshooting difficulty*

---

\*    *but have you read your Gertrude Stein?*

If to tremor is a wield or boy upon those girlish
fingers you do possess
Cathect an opening in my seal or frill a goad to leak
yr juice a prolect to confect a lettered syllable
upon my torpor a tress or "suddenly woke up", shouting

haunted by your hand & its wet curl beneath or in my core
"two slits" being an ontologic phrase
accepting the glint or sign of any aperture
to fecundate such an "any aperture"
wherein alterity's trace adheres

curious   harsh   curious

this image trust an arm yr shoulder's slip upon the bed
i saw your dearest wield, its just demeure
roar unto my article

i saw you


dear red boy

❖❖❖

*L*: "To give the essence of a proposition means to give the essence of all description, and thus the essence of the world."

*N*: "To have them separate is to move. Tying the pieces together
the question changed.

a reader"

*L*: "What *can* be shown, *cannot* be said."

*N*: "in the middle of me
watching her
becomes a proper noun"

*J-F*: ". . . narration ceaselessly produces history."

*N*: "Taking words and placing them in someone's mouth when the text requires something about necessity distinct from the facts."


❖❖❖

*L*: "Among the possible groups of truth-conditions there are two extreme cases."

*N*: "The rules apply only when she can see me. If it's happening over there and she can't see it. If I can't see it and it hasn't affected the conditions, but only when I think of it. It begins. And then thinking of it so begins to affect itself and become the conditions. . . .

assured and aroused"

## Archaic Torso of Kim

Beneath the lamp of my cheek's glow, in your hands I am
daring the rift of our angel. Against your torso
I bestow in my candles an impelled breath, a feature,
an opening of my shoes, what we both knew at first sight

could not be halted. We drew outward into the citadels
of the blended chest, drawing up what we had lent
our chest & the skin we caressed that night
of a young girl, we invented our sills over & over.

Have you read your Gertrude Stein? The curs
of the day come and torment us at distance,
a line twigged from Randall Jarrell.
Not even death can come to us now wearing shoes.

To hold thus is stellar, an impetus of mouths we liquored outward
into a night of stars until we soaked the lip, arraigned into each other's gaze.

You must change your life to Renate Rilke's.
You must rewrite *The Panther* of your frère Steve Rilke.
You must read your Frank O'Rilke now.
You must write a sonnet, right away,
(maybe).

You must ask Norma Cole if she has read her Gertrude Rilke.

You must ask if you may call her Norma Rilke.

❖❖❖

Go & read your Norma Cole.
Particules of sleep the lunge abeys follicular
amaze me now akimbo your west-most arm or field
wherein reside my archaic torso

a pale coin of a tressed anatomy released to gaze

your my drives that do attend so well to lust & thought
that crossing fire with tender impediment & skirts a lift to shine
admit twice-told its vesticulum
the thumb an entry turned the gaze we buckled to this forge
a trained impact in the mouth of stars
you enact in me & I in you
& you in me & I in you

r e n d e d   u n t o   B y z a n t i u m*


❖❖❖

*N*: "go inside and close
      scrubbed, blood pressure
      a warning to have more contact

      Leaves a torch which sets fire to the hedge."

*L*: "Propositions cannot represent logical form: it is mirrored in them.
What finds its reflection in language, language cannot represent. What
expresses *itself* in language, *we* cannot express by means of language."

*N*: "When I take your shape

      _____

      Just the image"


❖❖❖

---

\*     *the wet suck of yr palm folds up its clock into the arm's bent strut we incinerate as fuel*
      *rending time by space's brave will or intentionality*

## (My will)

Your hand's fraught interpretation calls forth deep affect
I could not anticipate but now
*may crave*
 Your gleam or suck a roar
 Your insist I am not ready & my resulting tome
 The leaf I show you turns
 Various artifacts appended to my "wrote accordingly"
 A spit I lay near whisper's source now wet upon your hair
 You surging upward into my arm or hum
 to bless or push against my shoulder it is "my"
 "chocar"
*to see its immediacy*
 wanting thus an able cathedral to go on
*makes it tighter*
 calls you out of shared gorgeous entry
 courses syllable our confect
 To defer

 the admired entry to concatenate
 a leaf may deign

*transitive to express a history of soil*
*or utopic soil in our very designation*
 your sweater torn off by my glance I will henceforth admit
 it was my glance that tore it
 pure expectation framed with welled biology

 impact a saturation to your leaf or dove
 a girlish note
*I'm ready*

*L:* "The world is independent of my will."

*L:* "Logic is not a body of doctrine, but a mirror-image of the world."

«J'ai grandi dans le livre. Je mourrai dans le livre. Je n'ai pas connu d'autres demeures . . .» disait-il. Et il ajoutait: «Je n'ai jamais levé les yeux du livre. »

Edmond Jabès, *Le Livre des ressemblances*

# Her Debits

## Thrum

An earlier "Thrum" is reproduced here for the curious reader. The 1364 was a dining car; this version is Eddy Joyal's. *"All my life, I thought, I'll remember this insane happiness."* That's not Eddy, but Jorge Semprún, from the end of *Literature or Life*.

There were charmed trespass we couldn't send

Gates that trembled over *omega*

Fortuity sembling a fond polestar

In our house a cuisine
spelled wrong
Horned in sideways

Trumped-up temerity
to endless *leave*
"you old conniver"

Where indigenous is a heartstroke from picturesque

A fond melody near me

When I craved melody's end, anoint
inscriptive


%


Unable -- henceforth --
To decry "facticity" in the line
where he entered through a sound door
the door frame squared off
perfectly
"& all that"

Fortuity is a candle that eludes regret?
Waiting for "both of us" to blunder through
(a doorway)
Basically -- impetuous --


%


Meeting, in a word, our homonyms
of exemplary endeavour
To wake up thinking
"the virus mendacious in a tomb"
the dreamed dog soft in my arms
skinless red, a meat curmudgeon
To dream your face is to
mesmerize infinitely
Whose curious soft eyes everywhere

thrum

%

As if a wilfulness infinitesimally forestalls regret
forestalls absence
"A dog fallen over sideways in a hug's fierce
hegemony"

a tune

sung aloud for "Irish voices"
meaning "there is a lilt"

"walking toward me laughing on Salem at Bloor"
"a gethsemane of indigence stole us"
"Eddy picking up *4 on 2* in the 1364"
"K's smile"

a neat reasonable blade of sunlight
's transversal

objectic
eidem

%

Where if an the opus corrupted enmity
Saying "gafas de sol"
would you believe it
at such a moment

"gafas de sol"

or frail misericordia
Did they want lament *(I don't think so)*
(it's a gay life ain't it)

*But to disseminate*

%

Which becomes gradually more narrational.
Out of the heart,
which has been dispensed with

*or not*

Or eased into joy
eased into "warm company"
then left suddenly alone
Looking up from the pale loam of the chest to the window

where they say

                "a fact of it"

                "the world lies[1]"

---
[1] confabulate  charms  incuses  herir

## Astro's House of Ripey Lyrick

was first published in December 1997 by Zat-So Productions in a handmade edition of 2 in CD covers, spiral-bound in red boards, with original pencil drawings and insert on thermal fax paper.

## The Red Archive

"The inability to sustain a home" could be a borrowed or misheard phrase from a session in July 1997 in Leeds, England, at the conference "Women, Texts, Communities, Technologies". *My notebook is obscure on this point; any correction or attribution is welcome.* Also, to "There is no place on earth without its beauty", my brother Kenneth Mouré noted: "One can't be completely categorical". To which I reply: "One can, and can't". As "Thrum" says: "Outside the window, the world lies".

## 7 Cues to the Instability of Artistic Order

Where there are facing pages with the left side in black type and the right in grey, the left side is "the written," and the right is a version or response text, not a faithful translation. It is also "written". Debts are owed to Colette St-Hilaire (the marvellous St.-Exupéry is her gift), Robert Majzels and Ginette de Montigny for help with French, and to Lisa Robertson who insisted on the piece for *Raddle Moon.*

## Spills Her A Notes on Wit

is indebted to a perverse reading (mine) of Alexander Pope's *An Essay on Criticism* (1711).

## Calor

owes debts to a constellation: Gilles Deleuze's *Logique de la sensation;* Robert Hughes' biography of Frank Auerbach, especially the progressive versions of the drawing "Portrait of Sandra 1973–74"; Yolande Racine's commentary on the history of portraiture in her abstract on *Hall of Shadows*, a Luc Courchesne video installation; Robert Majzels's sneeze when he read "Eschew?" and his other readings of this work-in-progress; Erin O'Brien, who was in Granada where the poem started; page XIV of John Randall's *Learning Latin;* the section on St. Augustine in *Reading Medieval Latin* and Bk 8.XII.28 of *The Confessions;* Bill Readings's *Introducing Lyotard;* Jean-François Lyotard's *Libidinal Economy* and *Discours, Figure;* Lisa Robertson's *Earth Monies*, a companion; and Ian Gibson's work on Federico García Lorca, wherein are the words of sculptor Eduardo Carreterra, who as a youth in Granada witnessed the arrest of Lorca, though at the time he did not realize what he'd seen: "*I retain a clear memory of afternoon light*".

**The Wittgenstein Letters to Mel Gibson's Braveheart**
holds words from San Francisco (via Toronto) poet Norma Cole. It also
listens to the philosopher Ludwig Wittgenstein, who insisted on conversing
with Norma. *The quotes can be traced as follows:*

Page 105    Norma Cole, *Mars* (Listening Chamber: Berkeley, 1994) 15
Page 107    Cole 61, 62
Page 108    Ludwig Wittgenstein, *Tractatus Logico-Philosophicus*
                (Routledge: New York, 1995) 6.54
                Cole 5
Page 109    Cole 81–2; Wittgenstein 4.126
Page 112    Wittgenstein 5.5303; Cole 87
                Wittgenstein 5.556; Cole 62
Page 113    Wittgenstein 2.014; Cole 90
                Wittgenstein 2.023
Page 115    Wittgenstein 4.463, 5.43; Cole 74
Page 117    Wittgenstein 5.4711; Cole 20
                Wittgenstein 4.1212; Cole 5
                Jean-François Lyotard, *Des dispositifs pulsionnels*
                (Union générale des éditions: Paris, 1973) 175
                Cole 5
Page 118    Wittgenstein 4.46; Cole 14
Page 119    Cole 4; Wittgenstein 4.121
                Cole 34
Page 120    Wittgenstein 6.373, 6.13

The title "(Socially-constituted objects include)" is an echo from Donna
Haraway's essay "A Cyborg Manifesto"; in the same optic, "(Bestows
profound benefits on her practitioner)" and "(Tremendous assertion)" echo
Rachel Rosenthal's performance *Taboo Subjects* from October 1981. "The
Wittgenstein Letters" is for Kim Fullerton, for whom it is *musical*, a musical,
amusing, in return for her deft amaze, and for the cherished beauty of her
proclamation. *14 March 1997 Montreal, Toronto*

**Some of the work in this and prior versions appeared in or has been
accepted for:**

CANADA
*Raddle Moon, Boo, The Capilano Review, Open Letter, Brick*
USA
*Poets' Calendar for the Millennium* (Sun & Moon Press),
*Mr. Knife, Miss Fork #2* (same),
*Denver Quarterly, 3 Girls Review, Mirage #4/Period(ical),*
*The East Village Poetry Web*
(http://www.geocities.com/~theeastvillage)
UK
*the text, language alive, TEST digital projection project* (www.test.org.uk)

This book owes much to the acuity and encouragement at different times of Norma Cole, Kim Fullerton, Robert Majzels, and Lisa Robertson. Special thanks to Lou Nelson and to Ken Mouré, whose constancy in friendship makes "it" possible. Thanks to Spinoza via Deleuze. To Joanne Page, who lent the cottage where I finished the (a) book. To the people who first published this work. To Adrienne Leahey and Paula Krulicki of Anansi for brilliant collaboration on typesetting and layout, especially where there are drawings or abraded text. To Emeren García for taking that flight from Madrid right over Orense and Santiago. To Astro Fullerton, cat extraordinaire. And to my editor Robert Majzels, for his absolute concern for detail and echo, for many insistences, and for making sure I didn't wreck it. "Tentative" does equal "beautiful" in this formulation, Robert.

Important thanks to Kim Fullerton, whose fervid intelligence and art commotions have brought me many openings and make me "think again". *Plus I would have surely drowned without the kitchen tent.*

Without the support of senior arts grants from The Canada Council and from Le Conseil des arts et des lettres du Québec, this work would, quite bluntly, not exist. I thank both councils for their crucial role in making its presence possible.

*"What starts as a figure
where they say doubt lives
can become a woman
years later"*

* * * * * * * * * * * * * * * * * * * * * * * * * * * * * * * * * * * * * * * * * * * * * * * * *

This book is for the changes, and for the grace with which we lived them. *"Las cosas que se van no vuelven nunca, / todo el mundo lo sabe, / y entre el claro gentío de los vientos / es inútil quejarse."* F.G.L.

Erin Mouré
May 1998
Le Rachel-Julien, Montréal